COOL

CRIME SCENE BASICS

Securing the Scene

ESTHER BECK

ABDO
Publishing Company

VISIT US AT WWW.ABDOPUBLISHING.COM

Published by ABDO Publishing Company, 8000 West 78th Street, Edina, Minnesota 55439.
Copyright © 2009 by Abdo Consulting Group, Inc. International copyrights reserved in all countries.
No part of this book may be reproduced in any form without written permission from the publisher.
The Checkerboard Library™ is a trademark and logo of ABDO Publishing Company.

Printed in the United States.
Design and Production: Mighty Media, Inc.
Art Direction: Kelly Doudna
Photo Credits: Kelly Doudna, Ablestock, iStockPhoto (Bonnie Jacobs), ShutterStock
Series Editor: Pam Price
The following manufacturers/names appearing in this book are trademarks: Ace, Eveready, Kodak,
Mead, Sharpie, Stanley, Sterling. Google, Google Maps, and the Google Logo are trademarks of
Google Inc. Map imagery © 2008 DigitalGlobe.

Library of Congress Cataloging-in-Publication Data

Beck, Esther.
  Cool crime scene basics : securing the scene / Esther Beck.
     p. cm. -- (Cool CSI)
  Includes index.
  ISBN 978-1-60453-484-9
  1. Crime scene searches--Juvenile literature. 2. Forensic
sciences--Juvenile literature. I. Title.

  HV8073.8.B432 2009
  363.25'2--dc22
                        2008023816

TO ADULT HELPERS

You're invited to assist up-and-coming forensic investigators! And it will pay off in many ways. Your children can develop new skills, gain confidence, and do some interesting projects while learning about science. What's more, it's going to be a lot of fun!

These projects are designed to let children work independently as much as possible. Let them do whatever they are able to do on their own. Also encourage them to keep a CSI journal. Soon, they will be thinking like real investigators.

So get out your magnifying glass and stand by. Let your young investigators take the lead. Watch and learn. Praise their efforts. Enjoy the scientific adventure!

CONTENTS

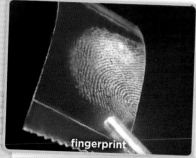
fingerprint

shoe print

fibers

FUN WITH FORENSICS

So you want to know more about crime scene investigation, or CSI. Perhaps you saw a crime solvers show on television and liked it. Or maybe you read about an ace investigator in a favorite **whodunit** book. Now you're curious, how do the investigators solve crimes?

The answer is *forensic science*. This term means science as it relates to the law. The many areas of forensic science can help link people to crimes, even if there are no eyewitnesses. Forensic scientists look at the evidence left at a crime scene and try to figure out what happened there.

tool marks

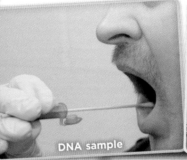
DNA sample

chemical residue

Evidence can include fingerprints, shoe prints, and fibers. It can include DNA samples from blood and saliva, tool marks, and chemical residue. Often this evidence can be quite small. In the CSI business, this is known as trace evidence. But even the smallest evidence can place a suspect at a crime scene.

Crime scene investigators **analyze** the evidence. Then they try to answer these questions about a crime.

1. What happened?
2. Where and when did it occur?
3. Who are the suspects, and why did they do it?
4. How was the crime done?

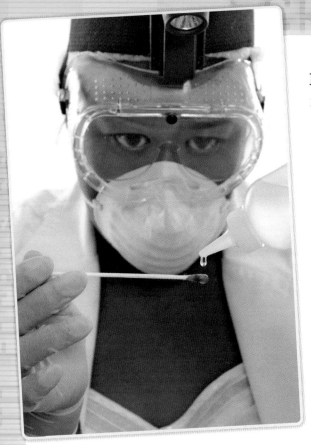

Different kinds of evidence require different kinds of scientists to find the answers to these questions. Forensic scientists specialize in fields such as chemistry, biology, physics, engineering, psychology, and even **entomology** and **botany**.

All these scientists use common sense and old-fashioned observation. They also rely on high-tech equipment and the latest scientific discoveries. Most important, forensic scientists use the scientific method.

Investigators begin by observing the crime scene. They then predict what happened and, if possible, who committed the crime based on the evidence.

Next they test the evidence. Their test results may support their predictions. Or, the results may tell them that their predictions were not correct.

Finally, they draw a conclusion about what happened. They may decide that further testing is required.

In this book series, you'll have a chance to test your own crime-solving talent. You'll do some challenging hands-on forensics activities. Each book in the series covers a specific area of CSI. In addition to this book, *Cool Crime Scene Basics: Securing the Scene*, be sure to check out:

- *Cool Biological Clues: What Hair, Bones, and Bugs Tell Us*
- *Cool Eyewitness Encounters: How's Your Memory?*
- *Cool Forensic Tools: Technology at Work*
- *Cool Physical Evidence: What's Left Behind*
- *Cool Written Records: The Proof Is in the Paper*

Altogether, these books show how crime scene investigators use science to **analyze** evidence and solve crimes.

Whoduzit in Whodunits: Forensic Psychologists

Psychologists study minds and behavior. Forensic psychologists study the minds and behavior of crime suspects. They try to determine motive, or why a person may have committed a crime. They may try to determine whether a person was sane when he or she committed a crime.

CSI LAB

THE SCIENTIFIC METHOD

Forensic scientists aren't the only ones who use the scientific method. All scientists do.

The scientific method is a series of steps that scientists follow when trying to answer a question about how the world works. Here are the basic steps of the scientific method.

1. Observe. Pay attention to how something works.

2. Predict. Make a simple statement that explains what you observed.

3. Test. Design an experiment that tests your prediction. You need a good idea of what data to gather during the test. A good test has more than one trial and has controlled variables.

4. Conclude. Compare the data and make a conclusion. This conclusion should relate to your prediction. It will either support the prediction or tell you that your prediction was incorrect.

COOL CSI JOURNAL

Taking notes is important when you collect evidence as a crime scene investigator. Writing down facts helps crime scene investigators remember all the details of a crime scene later, when a crime is tried in court.

At the beginning of each activity in this book, there is a section called "Take Note!"

It contains suggestions about what to record in your CSI journal. You can predict what you think will happen when you test evidence. And you can write down what did happen. Then you can draw a conclusion.

As you do experiments, record things in your journal. You will be working just like a real forensic scientist.

TAKE NOTE!

Get out your CSI journal when you *see* this box. "Take Note!" may have questions for you to answer about the project. There may be a suggestion about how to look at the project in a different way. There may even be ideas about how to organize the evidence you find. Your CSI journal is the place to keep track of everything!

SAFE SCIENCE

Good scientists practice safe science. Here are some important things to remember.

- Check with an adult before you begin any project. Sometimes you'll need an adult to buy materials or help you handle them for a while. For some projects, an adult will need to help you the whole time. The instructions will say when an adult should assist you.

- Ask for help if you're unsure about how to do something.

- If something goes wrong, tell an adult immediately.

- Read the list of things you'll need. Gather everything before you begin working on a project.

- Don't taste, eat, or drink any of the materials or the results unless the directions say that you can.

- Use protective gear. Scientists wear safety goggles to protect their eyes. They wear gloves to protect their hands from chemicals and possible burns. They wear aprons or lab coats to protect their clothing.

- Clean up when you are finished. That includes putting away materials and washing containers, work surfaces, and your hands.

COOL CRIME SCENE BASICS: SECURING THE SCENE

The first step of solving a crime scene investigation is to secure the scene. You may know that police mark off a crime scene with yellow tape that reads "Do Not Cross." This tape keeps people from disturbing the crime scene while investigators gather evidence.

INE DO NOT CROSS   POLICE LINE DO NOT CROSS   POLICE

It's important to keep down the number of people at a crime scene. Newcomers can accidentally destroy evidence. Or they can bring in materials that might be mistaken for evidence. It's also important that people who might have seen the crime stay until police have interviewed them.

Deciding what area is part of a crime scene can be complicated. Crime scenes come in all shapes and sizes. And they often include more than one site. **Staging** areas are where criminals planned and prepared for their crimes. Primary scenes are where the crimes happened. Secondary crime scenes, such as get-away cars, are the places criminals went after the primary scene. All of these spots are considered part of the crime scene.

So exactly who works a crime scene? In general, crime scene investigators fit into two camps. Field analysts gather evidence at the actual crime scene. Laboratory analysts run experiments on the evidence back at the crime lab. A crime lab is a special facility with all the scientific gear needed to run forensic tests.

Evidence is anything that can help determine whether a crime has occurred. Investigators collect evidence at a crime scene. They lift fingerprints, gather hair and fiber samples, take photos, and make detailed notes. They bag and label the evidence and transfer it to the crime lab.

Crime scene investigators carefully document the crime scene. This helps them keep track of the process of clearing it. Their notes often include sketches and photographs of the area. Crime scene records also include the name of every person allowed in and out of the scene.

THE LOCARD EXCHANGE PRINCIPLE

This fancy-sounding rule is the simple idea behind all forensic science. The rule is named for French police officer Edmond Locard. He was the first to notice that any contact with another person, place, or thing causes an exchange of materials.

For example, when you relax on a sofa, you probably leave behind fibers from your clothing or hairs from your head. And small fibers from the sofa probably stick to your clothing and head! In other words, there's an exchange of materials. Of course, you don't normally notice this exchange. But if investigators look for the fibers, there's a good chance they'll find them!

MAKE A CSI KIT

First things first. In this activity, you'll create a simple CSI kit to use when investigating crimes. After all, an expert crime solver needs the right tools!

MATERIALS

- large shoebox or small plastic box with cover
- paints or markers to decorate the box
- paintbrushes
- magnifying glass
- flashlight

- plastic zipper bags
- tweezers
- latex gloves
- shoe covers
- pencil and notebook (your CSI journal will do)

- camera and film (a disposable camera will work) or a digital camera
- crime scene tape (blue painter's tape or a colorful crepe paper ribbon from a party store will work)

TAKE NOTE!

Keep a "grocery list" in your CSI journal. Note the supplies you run out of or need to add for future activiti...

1. Decorate the box any way you like. But remember, investigating a crime scene is serious business.

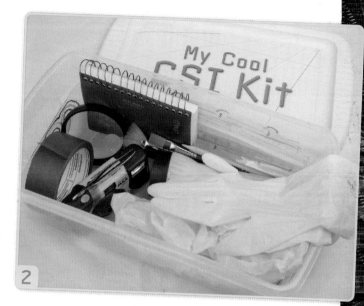

2. Place the items on the materials list in the box. Try to organize the box so that you can get to the supplies easily.

2

3. Remember to replace the items as you use them.

THINK CSI

For crime scene investigators, CSI kits include the tools of the trade. Specialists, such as fingerprint examiners, might even have more than one kit ready to go at all times. The first kit has all the basic tools they use on a regular basis. A second kit stores materials needed for more unusual tests.

CSI TIP

A professional crime scene investigator's toolkit includes other supplies, such as a serology kit for collecting blood. However, the basic CSI kit you put together here is fine for many of the projects in this book series. As you work through the activities, you can add other supplies. Always remember to keep your kit well supplied and organized. Then it will always be ready for your next investigation.

MAP IT!

THE CRIME SCENE: You enter your bedroom after school to find that your diary has disappeared. Before you blame anyone, stop and think. What exactly happened here? Mapping the crime scene could help you **analyze** the crime.

Crime scene investigators write notes and take photographs of the crime scene. They also make a simple map of the area. This sketch helps them recall the basic layout of the scene. It shows where evidence was located. In this activity, you'll practice mapping a crime scene, just as real investigators would do in the field.

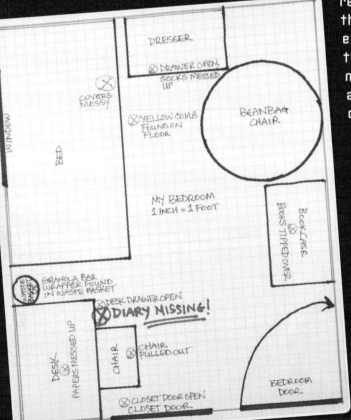

MATERIALS

- paper (can be graph paper)
- pencil
- eraser
- retractable tape measure

TAKE NOTE!

Don't forget to use your CSI journal to store your field notes and sketches.

1. Measure the dimensions of your room. Start by measuring each wall. If your room is box shaped, measure its length and width only. If your room has a **unique** shape, measure each wall.

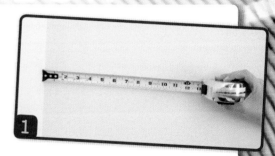

2. Notice the room's angles. If the corners are standard 90-degree angles, your task will be easy. If the angles are smaller or larger than 90 degrees, your task might be trickier!

Think CSI

Field analysts are often responsible for mapping a crime scene. A well-drawn map, detailed notes, and photographs all help investigators determine what happened. This information will help build a solid **case** that will stand up in court.

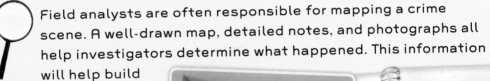

3. Draw a scale model of your room. First decide the scale you will use. For example, if your room is 12 feet (3.7 m) by 14 feet (4.3 m), you might want to use a one-inch scale or a five-centimeter scale. On the map, one inch equals one foot or five centimeters equals one meter.

4. Draw the basic shape of your room on the paper.

5. Add details to your room map. Draw windows, doors, closets, and large pieces of furniture. Be sure to use the same scale you used to draw the rest of your room. Use the sample crime scene map on page 18 as a guide.

6. Place an X on the map where the missing item would normally sit. Also include any evidence you found. Ask an adult for help if you get stuck.

MORE MAP FUN

MATERIALS

- access to a computer with an Internet connection
- paper
- eraser

THE CRIME SCENE: When you leave school at the end of the day, you find that your bike isn't where you left it. Other kids are standing by the bike rack looking for their wheels.

Then a kid yells from down the street. His bike has turned up in the bushes. You all run down the block to look for your bikes. Bikes begin to show up in the craziest places. What's going on here? Is this a crime or someone's idea of a joke?

Not all crime scenes are a single room. In fact, crime scenes can be as small as a laptop computer or as large as several city blocks. In this activity, you'll use Google Maps to locate an aerial view of your school block. Then you'll sketch a map of the scene.

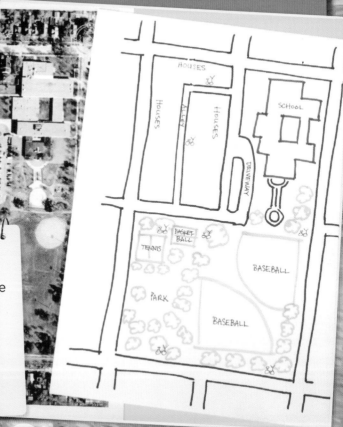

TAKE NOTE!

Keep a list of places to look up on Google Maps. Try to find buildings, such as your house or apartment building. *Also* look for open places, such as a nearby park. Do these places look familiar from this point of view? Which sites do you think would make complicated crime scenes?

1. With an adult helper, visit http://maps.google.com. This Web site lets you look at a map or an aerial view of any address. The aerial pictures are taken from **satellites** orbiting high above the earth.

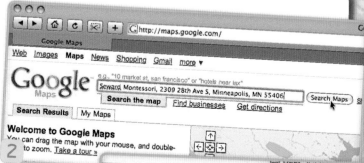

2. Type the address of your school in the "Search the map" field. Then click the "Search Maps" button.

3. Be patient as Google Maps locates your school.

4. Click the "Satellite" button to switch to the aerial photo view. Use the zoom feature to find a clear view of your school and the surrounding area.

5. Sketch a map of the area. Place small bicycles on the map in areas you think a thief or a jokester might hide bikes.

6. Don't worry about scale. This activity is designed just to get you thinking about the relative size of crime scenes.

5

THINK CSI

Experienced crime solvers know that the size of a crime scene doesn't always match how long it takes to process it. For example, it can take longer to examine a computer than a huge field. Investigators need to examine each site thoroughly, no matter what size it is. A public crime scene, such as a shopping mall or a train station, might involve many eyewitnesses. They all must be interviewed, so it will take longer to clear the **case**.

computer hard drive

tire tracks

POLICE LINE DO NOT

public place

PATTERN MAKES PERFECT

MATERIALS

- a small item such as a button, a die, or a coin
- at least two friends

THE CRIME SCENE: Everyone is in a panic! Your grandmother can't find her wedding ring. She remembers taking it off at your house to wash dishes. So where could it be?

You all spend two hours helping her search. Then your dad comes home from work and looks. There's a method to his search. He finds the ring in five minutes! So how'd he do it?

In this activity, you'll practice patterns for searching crime scenes. Investigators use these patterns when looking for evidence. Patterns keep the search orderly and can help locate small bits of evidence.

1. Choose a room or an outdoor space to be your crime scene.

2. Choose one person to hide the small item.

3. Read about the search patterns in "Think CSI" on page 25. Have the second person choose a search pattern and look for the item.

TAKE NOTE!

Make a table in your CSI journal to track how well each pattern works for each finder. Here is a sample chart.

Pattern	Time lapsed	Notes
Spiral		
Strip		
Grid		
Zone		
Pie		

4. Time how long it takes this person to find the object using each pattern. Make a table like the one in "Take Note!" Fill it in as you work.

5. Have the hider re-hide the small item after each find.

6. Take turns so you each get to hide and find. Be sure to keep a table for the second finder as well. Try to use a different pattern for each search.

7. Compare notes. What did you learn about the search patterns?

EVEN MORE TO EXPLORE

Get creative. Can you think of any other search patterns that might be useful? Design your own pattern and draw it in your CSI journal. Then try it, using the same method you did when filling the table. How did it work?

THINK CSI

Spiral. Circle from the center of the scene out. Or circle from the outside of the scene in. The spiral pattern is useful if you have only a few investigators at the scene.

Strip. Divide the search area into parallel strips. A team of investigators walks side-by-side in the same direction.

Grid. Divide the search area into perpendicular strips to create a grid. Teams of investigators walk side-by-side in these crossing directions. This is a good pattern if you have lots of people and a large area to search.

Zone. Split the area or room into equal-size zones. Each zone is assigned to a searcher. This pattern is good when searching very large areas or when looking for very small evidence.

Pie. Divide the crime scene into slices, similar to slicing a pie. Within each slice, the same or different search patterns can be used. This pattern is useful if the area is very large with different kinds of evidence.

STAGE A CRIME SCENE

THE CRIME SCENE: You work for a busy forensics unit. Two petnappings were reported in the same apartment building at the same time. Two teams are assigned to the investigations.

You and the other field analysts arrive to process the crime scenes. Your precise fieldwork could help crack the **case**. Did the same person commit the crimes? Or was there more than one petnapper?

In this activity, you and your friends will work in teams. You will make fake crime scenes for each other to investigate. Your CSI teams will collect evidence and catalog it, just like real crime scene investigators.

I have sophie the dog. If yo want to play with her, leave three cinnamon rolls outside Mike's door.
P.S. Please hurry. I'm hungry!

TAKE NOTE!
Documenting fieldwork is an important part of processing a crime scene. Keep a thorough list in your CSI journal of all the evidence your team uncovered at the **staged** crime scene.

MATERIALS

- CSI kit(s) as made on pages 16–17
- human hairs pulled from a hairbrush
- pet hairs from a pet bed or a pet brush
- paper and pencil or a computer and printer
- sand, baby powder, or cornstarch in a shallow box
- lip gloss
- glass or cup
- strings or fibers, from a piece of clothing (be careful not to damage the clothes while gathering the fibers)
- two rooms for staging the crime scenes (be sure to ask an adult for permission before you begin)
- friends

1. Divide your friends into two teams. Each team should have at least two investigators on it.

2. Have each team meet in private to plan what evidence they will leave as part of the petnapping crime scene. Here are some ideas.

- **ransom** note
- pet hairs
- human hairs
- lip prints on the rim of a glass
- fingerprints on a glass
- footprints in the sand, baby powder, or cornstarch
- clothing fibers

fibers

fingerprints

have Sophie the dog. If you want to play with her, leave three cinnamon rolls outside Mike's door.
P.S. Please hurry! I'm hungry!

ransom note

human hair

pet hair

lip print

3. Once each team has made their plan, have them prepare the evidence and **stage** the crime scenes. You can set a time limit for this part of the activity so it stays on track!

4. Switch rooms and have each CSI team process the crime scene the other team created. Take your work seriously. Remember, somebody's pet is depending on you!

5. Take notes, including lists of eyewitnesses. Draw crime scene maps. Put all the evidence in plastic bags and label them.

I have Sophie the dog. If you want to play with her, leave three cinnamon rolls outside Mike's door.

P.S. Please hurry. I'm hungry!

5

6. Now have each team present its evidence to the team that created the crime scene. How did you do? In a real crime situation, your work would be ready to send to a crime lab for **analysis**. Did your team miss anything?

WHICH CAME FIRST, FIELD ANALYSIS OR CRIME LAB ANALYSIS?

Which came first, the chicken or the egg? Which came first, field analysis or crime lab analysis? It can be tricky to think about field analysis without knowing more about forensic lab analysis. You will learn more about the many areas of forensic science in the other books in this series. After you do, try staging crime scenes again. You might even have your own ideas for evidence to plant!

CSI Tip

Sometimes criminals stage crimes to cover up what actually happened. A good example is a fire. A criminal might start a fire to cover up the evidence of a crime. The fire is also a crime, but it's staged, or fake.

Think CSI

In this activity, you performed the basic job of a crime scene field analyst. After the evidence is collected, crime lab analysts test the evidence in a crime lab. For example, they might test hair samples and fingerprints taken from the crime scene. In addition, forensic scientists with special skills, such as document examiners, might be called in.

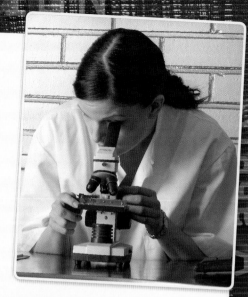

Whoduzit in Whodunits: Evidence Custodians

Evidence **custodians** are responsible for processing, transporting, and storing evidence. They take care of the evidence when it's in their custody. They also keep records of the chain of custody. That means they note who has the evidence and when and where they take it. For example, they record when evidence is checked out to be used at a trial.

Evidence custodians must be organized and trustworthy. They must take their jobs seriously. Crime victims and those accused of crimes depend on evidence to make their **cases** in court.

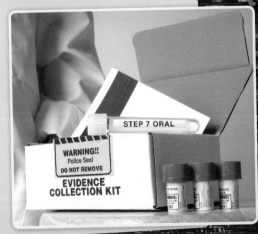

CONCLUSION

The activities described in this book are the basic steps of crime scene **analysis**. They are similar to the steps investigators follow when processing a crime scene.

- Provide first aid to anyone hurt during the crime.

- Decide the basic area of the crime scene.

- Secure the scene, using tape to prevent unauthorized people from randomly exiting and entering it.

- Take statements from eyewitnesses while they are still in the area.

- Process the evidence at the scene, carefully collecting and labeling it.

- Release all the evidence to the evidence **custodian**.

The field analysis done at a crime scene is just the beginning of a longer process. Forensic scientists will continue to **analyze** it in the lab. So it's very important that field analysts do trustworthy work.

Remember, every crime scene is **unique**. Even after years of practice, investigators can still run into complications when processing scenes. That's part of what makes CSI work so interesting!

GLOSSARY

analysis – the identification or study of the parts of a whole.

analyze – to study the parts of something to discover how it works or what it means.

botany – the study of plants.

case – a situation requiring investigation and consideration by police. Also, the set of arguments made by a lawyer in a court of law.

custodian – someone who protects and takes care of something.

entomology – the study of bugs.

ransom – money demanded for the release of someone or something held captive.

satellite – a manufactured object that orbits the earth.

stage – to prepare for and cause an event such as a sporting event or a play to happen. Because the word *stage* is related to theater, it sometimes refers to something that is faked, or made to appear real when it is not. A staging area is where people get everything ready for an event.

unique – being the only one of its kind.

whodunit – a slang word meaning detective story or mystery story.

INDEX